SKATING WHERE THE PUCK WAS

The Correlation Game in a Flat World

WILLIAM J. BERNSTEIN
© 2012

ISBN-10: 0988780305

ISBN-13 9780988780309

Ebook design by Reality Premedia Services Pvt. Ltd.

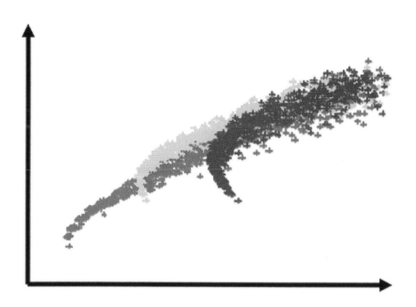

Skating Where the Puck Was: The Correlation Game in a Flat World is the second installment in the Investing for Adults series. This series is not for novices.

This booklet explores the notion that, as a general rule, no magic policy rich in high-return/low-correlation alternative asset classes exists that will simultaneously preserve upside reward and protect against downside losses. And as long as I'm lowering your expectations, this booklet is most certainly not a blueprint for the "perfect portfolio." You're an adult, after all, so you know that the future efficient frontier lies well beyond our ken; presumably you already know all about the mechanics, long-term benefits, as well as the uncertainties, of wide diversification and factor tilt using low-cost, efficient vehicles and the risk/reward spectrum between all-fixed-income and all-equity portfolios. Rather, this booklet provides a way of navigating a global investment landscape that grows ever more linked by the month, and a way of thinking about diversification.

INTRODUCTION

Long, long ago in a financial universe far, far away, there lived an asset class so obscure and so far out of the purview of ordinary investors that it did not waltz to the same capital market tunes that serenaded the rest of the world; it seemed, rather, to dance to its own drummer, zigging when its peers zagged, and zagging when the others zigged. Even better, its returns exceeded those of conventional equities.

Sadly, the wonders of modern communication technology and financial intermediation penetrated into the remote securities valley where it dwelled, and just like the charming Balinese artist's village your parents first came across in the 1960s, it was overrun by the hordes.

Call this mythical asset class "International REITs," which over the past two decades has suffered this gruesome fate:

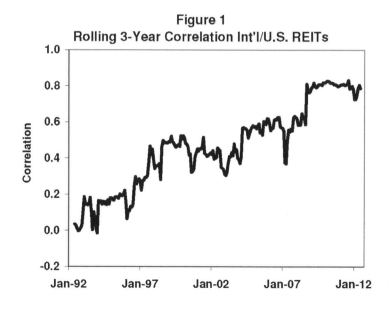

Figure 1
Rolling 3-Year Correlation Int'l/U.S. REITs

Elders of the investment tribe long enough in tooth will recall the refrain of a popular song from the distant 1970s: "Call someplace paradise, kiss it goodbye." Well, the same is generally true of diversifying asset classes: as soon as a new one gets discovered, it's already gone.

As indeed turns out to be the case with the market's current great white hope, "alternatives."

FALL FROM GRACE

In 2000, Yale Endowment manager David Swensen wrote a brilliant, influential book, *Pioneering Portfolio Management*, in which he proposed a portfolio strategy radically different from the traditional 60/40 stock/bond institutional model. Swensen deployed less than half his portfolio in conventional publicly traded foreign and domestic stocks and bonds, and invested the rest in less liquid assets: hedge fund strategies, private equity, private real estate, and commodities futures.

His strategy worked brilliantly; in the twenty years between July 1987 and June 2007, he clocked a 15.6% annualized return, 4.8% higher than the S&P 500. Better yet, along the way, the endowment experienced considerably less volatility. Good news traveled fast, and by 1997, the Princeton, Harvard, and Stanford endowments had copied Yale's trajectory into the alternatives universe.

As a dismal but useful rule, most good investment ideas eventually get run into the ground. By the mid 2000s, *tout le monde* had adopted the "Yale Model"; as of mid-2011, the 823 large endowments tracked by the National Association of College and University Business Officers invested an average of 53% of their funds in the "alternatives" pioneered by Swensen, as did most large public and corporate pension funds.

Were they happy that they did? The answer depends on their time frame. Over the ten years ending mid-2011, the university endowments, on average, barely nudged out a simple 60/40 mix of S&P 500/Barclays/Lehman Aggregate Bond bogey or the Vanguard Balanced Index Fund, which mimics this mix. But as more money has crowded into the alternatives arena, the university endowments began to fall behind; over the past 5- and 3-year periods ending mid-2011, the simple benchmarks listed above beat the average endowment. This pattern of evolving asset-bloat-caused deterioration is one also seen with hedge funds, commodities funds, and, unfortunately, with the Yale Endowment itself.[1]

First, hedge funds: Between the inception of the Hedge Fund Research group's widely based Global Returns series in January 1998 and the end of July 2012, the index returned 5.40%, versus 4.29% for the much riskier S&P 500.

So far, so good. As you can see in the first row of the below table, its 3-Factor stats (the first row, in bold) for the whole period are not too shabby:

Table 1. **Three-factor analysis of the HFR's Global Returns series, 1998–2012.**

Period	Ann'd alpha	MRK	SmB	HmL
1/98-7/12 (whole period)	**+1.8%**	**0.21**	**0.09**	**0.05**
1/98-12/02	+9.0%	0.15	0.12	0.05
1/03-12/07	-0.7%	0.31	0.06	0.07
1/08-7/12	-4.5%	0.34	0.09	0.07

Next look at the last three rows, which divide 1998–2012 into approximately equal subperiods. These clearly show deteriorating performance; during the first subperiod, the average hedge fund delivered 9% of annualized risk-adjusted outperformance, but by the last, it lagged by 4.5% per year. In fact, over the past 10 years, your money would have been better off in T-bills.

There are only so many billions of dollars of alpha in the world. Imagine, for example, that $1 billion of such excess returns are available to a given strategy, and further imagine that the average hedge fund incurs $10 million in annual commissions and market impact costs. (An efficient markets purist would argue that the market, as a whole, contains zero gross alpha. In this case, just assume that the above $1 billion figure represents the maximum opportunity offered up by dumb investors.) The first hedge fund using this strategy thus has the potential to make its managers and investors $990 million dollars; if manager fees siphon off one third of this alpha, then by the 67th fund, there is none left for the investors, and by the 100th fund, none remains for anyone. Beyond that, the average alpha grows ever more negative.

This is precisely what happened to hedge funds sometime in the early 2000s. Before that time, when only a relatively small number of funds were chasing their respective strategies, their average net harvest was still positive. But as total hedge fund assets sailed past a trillion dollars in the mid-2000s, the alpha commons got overgrazed, and the hedgie's increasing transactional costs and egregious fees overwhelmed the increasingly slim per-fund pickings. The swan dive in hedge fund performance is best demonstrated by plotting the trailing 5-year annualized returns of the Hedge Fund Research Global Index versus that of a simple equivalent-risk portfolio consisting of a 25/75 mix of the CRSP 1-10 Universe index and 1-month T-bills:

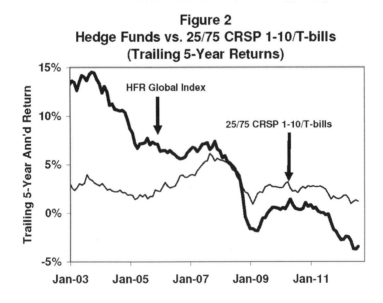

Figure 2
Hedge Funds vs. 25/75 CRSP 1-10/T-bills
(Trailing 5-Year Returns)

The same experience has also bedeviled commodities futures. In the late 1980s and early 1990s, many observers, most notably Roger Gibson, one of asset allocation's giants, noticed, like Swensen, that commodities exposure seemed to offer portfolio theory's version of the Immaculate Conception: high returns combined with low correlations with other standard portfolio components.[2] For example, between 1972 and 1990 (when Gibson wrote the first edition of *Asset Allocation*), the Markowitz grid of the Goldman Sachs Commodity Index (GSCI), the S&P 500, and long government bonds looked like this:

Table 2. **Markowitz Inputs for the GSCI, S&P 500, and Long Government Bonds, 1972–1990 (Annual Returns).**

	Return	SD	GSCI	S&P 500	Long Gov't
GSCI	16.26%	23.52%	1.00		
S&P 500	10.99%	17.50%	-0.37	1.00	
Long Gov't	8.49%	12.38%	-0.28	0.40	1.00

With higher returns than stocks and bonds and a negative correlation to both, how could you *not* add commodities exposure to your portfolio?

By now, you know the answer: just as with foreign real estate, before 1990, almost no actual U.S. portfolio managers *could*, let alone did, invest in commodities futures, because doing so involved, at least metaphorically and oft times actually, getting into all of the relevant pits, dressing in funny jackets, and jostling a scrum of sweaty, panicked ex-linebackers braying for money—or at least hiring a broker who did.

The difficulties of trading in commodities markets meant that prior to the twenty-first century, their major players were folks who were more concerned with simple survival than in collecting an attractive Markowitz grid, namely commodities producers for whom a fall in the price of crude oil or corn output in the months or years it took to get those products to market might prove catastrophic.

Put yourself in the position of an oil producer in the early 1980s. Crude is selling for $20 per barrel, and if that price falls to $12 or $15, you hope your bankruptcy lawyer knows his stuff. You'd like to sell your output six months down the road for the current $20 price. Who's going to take the opposite side of that futures contract at $20? No one. How about at $19.80? No takers. How about $19.60? Still no takers. Finally, a price of $19.40 entices a few commodities speculators from the sidelines. (It turns out that that the decision to hedge in the 1980s was a good short-term one, without which you would not have enjoyed the longer-term rise in prices.)

What just happened? Simple: the futures market produced a speculator willing to guarantee the current production price six months out in return for a 3% premium (the difference between $20.00 and $19.40). He or she knows that, all other things being equal, the price *should* remain the same, but there is a possibility that it will not. For bearing the risk that the price might fall, he or she will make, on average, a $0.60 profit on each contract when it expires.

Put another way, the speculator sold the producer an insurance policy against a fall in price. This phenomenon, in which the buyers of commodities futures earn an insurance premium, or "roll," is called "normal Keynesian backwardation," after the famous economist who first described the phenomenon in 1923. (Admittedly, backwardation is a somewhat simplified concept; buyers of oil, such as airlines and trucking companies, also wish to hedge by taking the opposite side of the trade. But, in general, the hedging needs of the sellers overwhelm those of the consumers in most commodities markets.)

Fast forward a quarter century; now the biggest players are the likes of Pimco and Oppenheimer, who have sold the gullible on the pre-1990 record of commodities futures—never mind that prior to 1990 this strategy had been, for all practical purposes, non-investible. Now who's the buyer of insurance? Answer: the biggest, and most motivated, players—mutual fund companies, pension funds, and wealthy private accounts. And who are now the lucky sellers? The producers, now in the fortunate position of being paid a positive roll on their short contracts. More importantly, what is being bought and sold by these behemoths? Answer: supposedly, protection against *inflation*, not deflation, as had been the case prior to 1990.

The two graphs below tell the sorry tale. Figure 3 shows the return of $1.00 invested in the Dow Jones-UBS Commodity Index in 1991, which simulates a long commodities futures strategy (the heavy line), and of the index of spot prices of the same commodities (the light line). Figure 4 displays the difference between these two curves—the cumulative roll return. Notice how before about 1998, with the dominant players insuring against deflation, normal Keynesian backwardation resulted, and the futures contracts outpaced the spot prices. After that point, though, as those seeking protection against inflation outnumbered those worried about deflation, the process reversed itself, and the spot price index started to underperform the futures index. The name for this unfortunate turn of events is not "forwardation," but rather, for etymologically obscure reasons, "contango."

Figure 3
Return of DJ-UBS Commodities Long/Spot

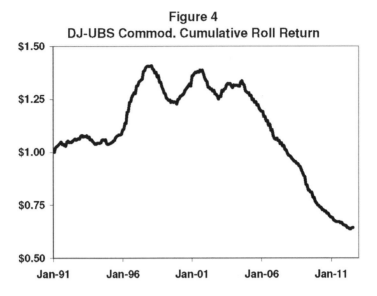

Figure 4
DJ-UBS Commod. Cumulative Roll Return

Pity the poor futures fund investor, who over the 2005–2012 period has seen the price of commodities double, yet reaped a near-zero return on the futures contracts. (Why, you might ask, can't you simply invest in the spot returns? Because doing so requires taking physical possession of the product itself, which accounts for the current popularity of precious metals, one of the few commodities for which this is practical.)

By the turn of the new century, then, one of the major reasons to own commodities futures—the roll return—had reversed with a vengeance.

During the 2007–2009 financial crisis, the other shoe, in the form of much higher correlations, dropped; commodities futures, rather than being a non-correlating "alternative" asset, saw price declines just as devastating as those in equities. Figure 5 shows how during the 2007–2009 crisis, the correlation between stocks, as represented by the S&P 500, and commodities futures had increased dramatically and has remained high since. The only saving grace is that the correlation between bonds, represented by the Barclays/Lehman Aggregate Index, and commodities has remained low. At the present time, then, the best that can be said about commodities futures is that they offset the risk of longer bonds, if that's an asset class that appeals to you.

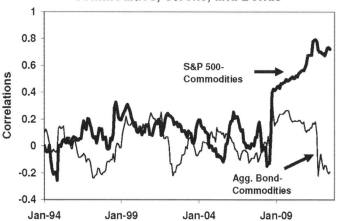

Figure 5
Rolling 3-Year Correlations among
Commodities, Stocks, and Bonds

To complete the picture, the traditional source of portfolio diversification, international equity exposure, has likewise tarnished; with increasing market globalization, the correlations among equities around the world have crept ever higher. In Figure 6, I've plotted the correlation of two emerging markets chosen at random, Turkey and Brazil.

Figure 6
Rolling 3-Year Correlation for Turkey/Brazil

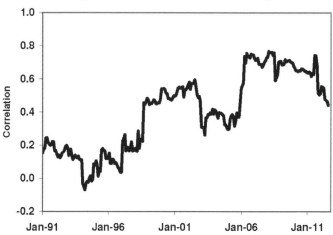

This, of course, makes perfect sense. Before 1995, far away, exotic markets were dominated by local players, and blood in the streets of São Paulo did not necessarily translate into financial turmoil in Istanbul. Today, things are very different; when bad news reaches John Q. Investor at the speed of light about Chile or China, he'll hit the sell button on his emerging markets fund; around the planet, Johannes Q., Juan Q., and Wang Q. Investor do the same thing. It matters not at all that companies in Malaysia and Mexico are doing just fine, thank you; as emerging markets funds shed assets, Malaysian and Mexican stocks get dumped along with those in China and Chile.

Finally, Figure 7 displays the trailing rolling 5-year correlation between the S&P 500 and EAFE indexes going back all the way to 1975 (the monthly data series started in 1970). It shows a curious picture, with low correlations prior to the mid 1990s, at which point an abrupt, sustained increase of correlations above 0.9 occurred. Exactly why this should have happened precipitously in the 1990s is anyone's guess, though the world financial turmoil triggered by emerging markets debt crisis seems the most likely suspect.

Figure 7
Rolling 5-Year Correlation for S&P 500/EAFE

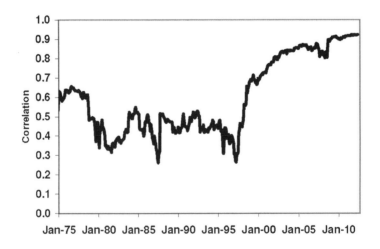

A bit of historical perspective is useful here. Before the First World War, international capital flows may have been as proportionately large as they are today; French and British capital financed many business ventures in both the United States and South America, especially railroad projects. The Great War put a crimp in that investment process, as did the rise in protectionism around the globe in the wake of the Depression, which brought crippling capital controls—at one point, English tourists could take no more than £50 out of the country. Not until the Bretton Woods regime broke down in 1971 did international investing begin to take off again. It may well be that a few decades were needed for international capital flows to gear up in the wake of the events of 1971, and until they did, international diversification consequently offered a substantial portfolio free lunch. Regrettably, the international buffet table is now bare, at least in terms of short-term risk reduction.

We've already seen how, before 2007, David Swensen tore up the track, but given the increasing correlations and decreasing returns of "alternative assets," how has the Yale Endowment done lately? Not so hot: for the five-year period between mid-2007 and mid-2012, it returned just 1.23% per year, versus +3.69% for the standard 60/40 S&P 500/ Barclays/Lehman Aggregate mix. Worse, Yale's exposure to alternatives didn't mitigate risk one single bit; for the 2008–2009 fiscal year, it lost a whopping 24.6%, about the same havoc wreaked by an ordinary all-stock portfolio and about twice the loss of the more conventional 60/40 mix. As put by academic Bruno Solnik, diversification fails us just when we need it most, and this goes in spades for illiquid alternative asset classes.

PIONEERING NO LONGER

The key word, then, in Swensen's book title was the first one: *pioneering.* It's almost impossible to find an endowment or high net worth private portfolio these days that is *not* thick with commodities futures, edge funds, real estate, and private equity. Even a casual reading of this booklet, though, reveals that simply investing in diversifying asset classes that have had salutary mean-variance characteristics in the *past* will not do; were that the case, then librarians would be the most successful portfolio managers. Rather, you have to own them before correlations rise and returns fall, as they usually do. (Yale, for example, virtually invented the concept of the absolute return hedge fund almost a generation ago; now that vehicle is about as cutting edge as Windows 95.)[3]

In short, you have to move on when you get too much company; the first people to invest in an asset class with high expected returns and low correlations enjoy sirloin, while the Johnny-come-latelys get hamburger. As succinctly put by Swensen, "Without creative portfolio choices, investment managers face dismal prospects since the old combination represents the consensus view."[4] Make no mistake about it; today, the Yale Model is most assuredly the "consensus view."

As the Yale endowment showed in 2008–2009, even David Swensen can get blindsided. In the 2000 edition of *Pioneering Portfolio Management*, he estimated the correlations of US equity with developed markets foreign equity, emerging markets equity, private equity, and real estate to be 0.60, 0.30, 0.40, and 0.15, respectively; by 2009 he had raised these estimates to 0.70, 0.60, 0.70, and 0.20. The 2009 edition seems to have been written before the Lehman failure, since it makes no mention of it or of any of the subsequent events, which revealed even his revised correlation estimates to have been optimistic.[5] In the foxholes, there are no mean variance enthusiasts.

Swensen certainly understood the potential flaws inherent in alternatives, especially when he saw others making the same mistake. In the 2000 version of his book, he criticized a paper published in the *Journal of Portfolio Management* purporting to show that commercial real estate had high historical returns and low correlations with other stocks, and thus deserved a very high portfolio allocation. Swensen asked,

> The fundamental flaw in [this paper] stems from failure to examine real estate return assumptions critically. Why should real estate be expected to return more than stocks and bonds? Why should real estate have lower risk than both stocks and bonds? Why should real estate exhibit negative correlation with stocks and bonds? Real estate contains characteristics of both debt and equity.[6]

The same could also be said about private equity and commodities. It is especially true of hedge funds, which are nothing more and nothing less than repackaged, and often leveraged, bundles of stocks, bonds, cash, real estate, and commodities; as such, how can they possibly behave radically different from the asset classes that comprise them?

The image of an ever more correlated investment universe evokes the thermodynamic concept of "heat death." This term was probably coined by Hermann von Helmholtz to express Lord Kelvin's vision of a universe in which free energy continuously dissipates and results in a bland, invariant state of maximal entropy. In investing terms, this corresponds to a cohort of nearly identically behaving asset class drones.

Will things really get that bad? We are, in fact, already there; further, it's *always* been that bad. As I've described above for several asset classes, the good old days never actually existed. Yes, international REITs were a wonderful diversifying asset, but the ordinary globally oriented investor, and even most extraordinary ones, did not have access to them before 2000. Ditto commodities futures before 1990 or, for that matter, foreign stocks before 1975 or so.

In short, the diversification opportunities available to ordinary investors were never as good as they appeared to be in hindsight. (Paradoxically, even in the face of increasing correlations among *asset classes*, as Burton Malkiel and his colleagues demonstrated in a 2001 *Journal of Finance* paper, correlations among *individual stocks* in the U.S. are actually decreasing. At the same time, they're also becoming more volatile, which means that the number of stocks needed to minimize portfolio volatility has increased from the traditional 20–30 to around 100.)[7]

MAKING THE BEST OF A BAD SITUATION

Is there hope for those desirous of diversification and superior returns in a nonsegmented financial universe? I can think of three possible routes to this goal:

- Be early.
- Be far-sighted.
- Be patient.

The first option—be early—is by far the hardest. We've already seen how David Swensen was first to the alternatives party, and how the Yale Endowment actually invented one of its parts—absolute returns strategy. Financial history provides an even more spectacular, and instructive, example of profitable earliness: John Templeton.

Born in 1912 the son of the only lawyer in a rural Tennessee town, he became its first resident to attend college: Yale. As the Depression deepened, his father could no longer pay his tuition, so he took to playing poker. He proved so adept that he found himself with extra cash to invest in stocks, a desire presumably inspired by the stellar Yale economics staff, which included the great Irving Fisher.[8] After completing a Rhodes Scholarship at Oxford in 1936, he traveled around the world with a friend, visiting, among other places, Japan.

After returning to New York in 1937, he began work at the brokerage firm Fenner and Beane (one of Merrill Lynch's many predecessors), then struck out on his own. Over the following decade, he made two sets of extraordinary equity purchases. The first was merely quirky: approximately $10,000 divided more or less equally among the 100 or so stocks trading on the New York and American exchanges for less than a dollar per share—including those in bankruptcy. Today, small-cap investing is as common as croissants and as easy as pushing a few buttons. Not so back then; Templeton's unusual stock universe was as absurdly cheap valuation-wise as it was expensive and difficult to buy, and he was only able to execute his purchases efficiently by calling in some favors from his old boss at Fenner and Beane. Needless to say, he earned high returns, quadrupling his investment within four years, effectively executing the small value strategy a half century before Fama and French described it.

His second prescient investment strategy was downright bizarre, at least for the time. Impressed by Japanese industriousness and the country's inexpensive equity markets during his world tour and in visits after World War II ended, he began making personal purchases of that country's stocks, then selling as cheaply as three times earnings. At first, his shares could not even be taken out of the country; now *that's* early.[9]

The rest, as they say, is history. He founded his own investment firm and started the first U.S. mutual fund—Templeton Growth—to invest extensively abroad; in 1970, Japanese equity constituted 60% of the fund. (The fund also held a fair chunk of the foreign real estate companies mentioned at the booklet's beginning.)

By 1979, Japan was no longer early enough for Templeton, and he began shifting assets back home to buy now-cheap domestic shares, by which point the fund had clocked a 20-year annualized return of 16.2%, versus 6.5% for the S&P 500. Sniffed Templeton about Warren Buffett: "Small-sighted . . . if he had spent more time in foreign nations, he would be better off."[10]

Since you're an investment adult, you know that the moral of the Templeton saga is *not* to seek out the next Templeton or Buffett; you're far more likely, of course, to get the next Bill Miller or Robert Sanborn. Rather, the Templeton story is a cautionary tale: once you think you've found a diversifying alternative asset, chances are you're already late to the ball. When private equity, timber, real estate, hedge funds, commodities futures, and David Swensen are on everyone's lips, if your portfolio looks like the Yale Endowment's, then you're likely to find yourself chairless when the music stops. Diversifying is easy; doing so early is difficult.

The next possible route to effective diversification—far-sightedness—is a bit easier. Resign yourself to the fact that during most bear markets, easily tradable risky assets—whether plain-vanilla stocks and bonds in 1955 or the entire panoply of exotic ETFs available today— move up and down nearly in sync. Even the likes of Warren Buffett and John Templeton lose money during such periods. Only occasionally do exceptions to universal bear market losses occur, usually when enthusiasm is largely confined to one corner of the investing universe, such as occurred during the late 1990s bubble in tech/large growth stocks, and during their subsequent burst in 2000–2002.

The most important boom/busts, though, result from the credit cycle, which was not the case in 2000–2002. Charles Kindleberger's epic *Manias, Panics, and Crashes* documented 46 of these credit-derived collapses between 1618 and 1998—about once every 9 years.[11] (Kindleberger died in 2003; the most recent bust began in 2007, precisely 9 years after the last one) When credit contracts during a crisis, investors reevaluate their risk tolerances, seek the comfort of government-secured vehicles, and dump their risky assets in order to do so—all of them.

The good news is that in reality, risk and diversification are about what happens over the long haul, not during a punishing downturn like 2007–2009, when the broad indexes lost more than 50%, and the riskiest asset classes, 70%; on a single day, October 19, 1987, the broad market indexes all fell by more than 20%. As I pointed out in the previous booklet in this series, *The Ages of the Investor*, the decade between January 1999 and December 2008 saw not one, but two, severe bear markets. During these ten awful years, the total nominal returns on asset classes ranged all the way from -13% for the S&P 500 to +251% for emerging markets value stocks. Now *that's* diversification. (It should be noted that all of the asset classes I listed in Table 1 of *Ages* were in fact available to investors as of 1999.)

So train yourself to think of risk not as the despondency you feel when your liquid net worth takes a sudden plunge, but rather as the possibility that you may find yourself unable to pay for life's necessities, particularly in your old age, or even more importantly, for your children's educations. Short-term and long-term risk are indeed two very different things. (Long-term thinking, unfortunately, may be more a matter of character than training; the parent who buys a Beemer and a 5,000 square foot house *before* he's secured his retirement and his kids' future college expenses may have already lost that particular game.)

This foregoing discussion of long- versus short-term risk would suggest that correlations among asset classes should decrease with an increasing measurement interval. Let's see if this is true. The longest possible baseline in this regard would be to look at various size- and value-sorted portfolios since 1926, a period that provides a more than eighty-year time horizon. The two least-related available asset classes should be the large growth and small value corners (Fama-French, including utilities). The correlation of monthly returns for these two asset classes for the 1927-2010 period was 0.77.

Next, let's look at correlations over a more mean-reversion friendly measurement interval, say 5 years. The average correlation for all five sets of overlapping 5-year measurement periods in Table 3 is 0.43; thus, the longest historical dataset of U.S. stock returns does indeed suggest that longer measurement intervals yield lower correlations.

Table 3. **Monthly versus 5-Year Correlations Of Fama/French LG and SV**

Period, Intervals	Correl.
1927–2010, Monthly Periods	0.77
1927–2006, 16 5-Year Periods	0.65
1928–2007, 16 5-Year Periods	0.62
1929–2008, 16 5-Year Periods	0.43
1930–2009, 16 5-Year Periods	0.22
1931–2010, 16 5-Year Periods	0.25
Average for 1927–2010 5-Year Periods	0.43

More importantly, and certainly more formally, Clifford Asness and his colleagues looked at international equity diversification over the past three decades and came to much the same conclusion. As they poignantly put it,

> Short-term crashes can be painful, but *long-term returns are far more important to wealth creation and destruction* . . .over the long term, markets do not tend to crash at the same time. This finding is no surprise because even though market panics can be important drivers of short-term returns, country-specific economic performance dominates over the long term. Diversification protects investors against the adverse effects of holding concentrated positions in countries with poor long-term economic performance.[12] [Italics added.]

Put yet another way, short-term risk is the sinking feeling you got in the pit of your stomach in late 2008 and early 2009; long-term risk is the potential for finding yourself, in the words of Ben Stein and Phil DeMuth, "pushing a shopping cart holding all your possessions down a wintry street and sleeping in doorways."[13] In short, resign yourself to the fact that diversifying among risky assets provides scant shelter from bad days or bad years, but that it does help protect against bad decades and generations, which can be far more destructive to wealth.

Finally, if you are patient enough, you don't need to be early, or even far-sighted. This booklet's main theme can be summarized as follows: when everyone owns the same set of risky asset classes, the correlations among them will trend inevitably towards 1.0.

But the converse is likely true as well; when an asset class falls out of favor, its ownership transfers from weak, herding hands into stronger and more independently minded ones, and correlations should fall along with rising future returns. Take, for example, precious metals equity (PME—the Ken French "gold" series), whose rolling 5-year correlation with the S&P 500 is plotted in Figure 8:

Figure 8
5-Year Rolling Correlation of PME/S&P 500

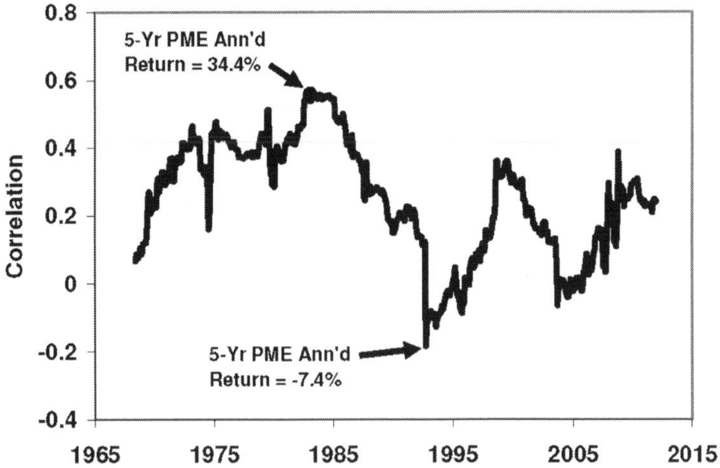

First note how, if anything, this correlation seems to be falling over time; its high point in the mid-1980s came at a time of enthusiasm for PME and was borne on high trailing returns. After that, the asset class went downhill for more than a decade, and with falling trailing returns came falling correlations, with a substantially negative correlation with industrial stocks by the early 1990s. Now that PME is back in favor, correlations have risen, and forward returns are likely to fall.

Who owned PME in the early 1990s? Stout-hearted, disciplined investors who knew that the asset class's miserable recent returns had produced compelling valuations, and, moreover, who would not sell out during a generalized rout. Who owned PME in the late 1970s (and who owns them now, as well)? Unsophisticated players with weak hands gulled by high prior returns who pushed the panic button when Mr. Market turned cruel that decade, thus raising PME's correlation with industrial equities.

To summarize: throughout all of financial history, it has been difficult, if not impossible, to invest in risky asset classes that are both highly liquid *and* short-term non-correlating, since liquidity, as we've seen, jacks up short-term correlations. In 1720, a French or English investor might have theoretically sheltered himself from the twin convulsions of the Mississippi Company and South Sea Company bubbles by investing in a Japanese or Chinese venture, but for the fact that the telegraph had not yet been invented, getting to the Orient was fraught with danger, and in any case both those nations were closed to Westerners (and everyone else, for that matter). In short, although it's difficult to be early, being patient is somewhat easier (though even that is no picnic, since buying an asset class after prolonged poor performance takes fortitude and a lot of spare cash); a long-term perspective usually pays off in the end.

Similarly, a generation ago, investors could have benefitted from the low correlations and high returns of commodities futures only by exerting the considerable effort of assembling and maintaining a wide variety of forward contracts. Are there such opportunities today? Of course. You can, if you so desire, gain salutary diversification benefits by moving to Orlando or Tucson and buying up foreclosures. The correlations with the rest of your financial assets will be low and the returns should be high, but so will be the effort and risks, among which will be playing landlord to possibly armed and/or drug-addled tenants. Remember, investing early in true alternative asset classes is, by definition, never easy, and once they do become securitized, liquid, and popular, all bets are off. In the digital age, any risky asset class you can buy with a keystroke can, and most likely, will bite you when things head south.

THE OLDEST DIVERSIFICATION

The Babylonian Talmud records, "And Rebbe Yitzchak said, A person should always divide his money into three: one third in land, one third in commerce, and one third at hand [silver]"; not bad investment advice for two millennia ago, and not bad for today. The modern version, first proposed by Harry Browne, adds a fourth category that didn't exist back then, long government bonds: thus, a 4 x 25 portfolio of bills, bonds, stocks, and physical gold. (For the purposes of this discussion, we'll use the 30-day T-bill, the Ibbotson long government bond, the CRSP 1-10, and bullion.) Here are the Markowitz inputs for annual returns between 1964 and 2011:

Table 4. **Markowitz grid for Harry Brown components (annual returns, 1964–2011)**

	Return	SD	CRSP 1-10	Long Gov't	Gold	T-Bill
CRSP 1-10	9.58%	17.74%	1.00			
Long Gov't	7.77%	11.84%	0.03	1.00		
Gold	8.15%	26.37%	-0.16	-0.20	1.00	
T-Bill	5.33%	3.00%	0.05	0.02	-0.01	1.00
Harry Browne	8.66%	7.55%	N/A	N/A	N/A	N/A

Not bad at all for the Harry Browne 4 x 25 portfolio (last row), you might say, particularly considering the fact that it lost just 1.31% in 2008. (Its largest nominal loss was 4.96% in 1981, which was worse than it appeared, since that year saw 8.94% inflation, for a real loss of 12.75%.)

Still, the Harry Browne portfolio looks too good to be true. What's wrong with this picture? Several things. For starters, gold was not easily investible during the first decade of this period; in fact, it was downright *illegal* to own the stuff from 1933 to 1974. Start the analysis in 1980, for example, and you were a full percent better off leaving it out of the portfolio entirely (i.e., owing one third stocks, bonds, and bills). Put another way, you can go off the gold standard and open up its ownership only once. It seems highly unlikely that gold will return several percent more than inflation in the coming decades; almost by definition, zero percent above inflation seems more like it. Next, compare the difficulty of purchasing and storing gold in, say, 1975 with the ease of buying a gold ETF today. (You're aware, of course, that GLD is, as of this writing, one of the world's largest ETFs.) If you've read this far, you realize that ease of purchase is a warning signal that the asset class in question's correlation with other risky assets has risen.

Likewise, the less than 2% gap that separated stock, bonds, and gold for 1964–2011 does not make any sense, and for much the same reason: The period, particularly its last half, saw a historic bull market in both bonds *and* gold, a pairing of events not likely to recur any time soon. Assume the same 4% inflation rate for the next several decades, and the returns of stocks look like they will fall slightly from 9.58% to around 7% (4% inflation plus 2% dividends plus 1% dividend growth), the returns of gold from 8.15% to 4%, the returns of long bonds from 7.77% to the current yield of 2.8%, and bills from 5.33% to God only knows what, but likely close to the assumed inflation rate of 4%. Average together all 4 of these numbers and you get an expected return of . . . 4.5%/0.5% nominal/real. You'll gain some return from rebalancing, but lose most of that to investment expenses. There will be tears.

So while I'll admit that the Harry Browne portfolio still has a lot to recommend it, I'm not sanguine about its current popularity, which rests on the salutary recent performance of its two most unorthodox risky components, gold and long bonds. Both investment history and human psychology suggest that when these two asset classes turn sour, as they will one day, Harry Browne adherents will abandon the approach in droves, as suggested by fund flows in and out of the Harry-Browne inspired Permanent Portfolio (PRPFX) over the past few decades.

*****

How, then, does the investor in today's flat world of hyperlinked markets approach asset allocation?

The prime directive of adequate diversification can be succinctly stated as follows: Your portfolio should not look like everyone else's. These days, that means the Yale Model—about half "conventional" stocks and bonds, and half "alternatives," whose prices have been bid into the stratosphere. In Wayne Gretzky-speak, as late as several years ago, David Swensen was still skating where the puck was going to be; now that the puck has arrived at the Yale Model, you want to skate somewhere else. The reason for this is simple: when everyone owns the same portfolio, a lot of those owners, especially the newcomers, are going to have weak hands, and when storm clouds gather, they're going to sell their risky assets indiscriminately and send correlations higher and returns lower, their prior salutary behavior be damned. If you own the Yale model, you are now skating where the puck was.

The best alternative asset class for the average investor may be in truly private investments, such as already mentioned, owner-managed (the owner being *you*) residential and commercial real estate in distressed markets, or in other private businesses in which you have special expertise. As previously pointed out, over the past few years, private investors have snapped up properties with expected triple net returns far higher, and correlations far lower with other assets, than can be obtained in the public markets. You most definitely *won't* get those benefits by purchasing a residential REIT with low single digit yields that will almost certainly crater during the next severe downturn. And those high returns and low correlations certainly won't be found in a Yale Model that is today being hawked by every wirehouse in town.

If you're unwilling to change professions and move to Orlando, then the best course is likely to float on the tide of liquid assets as successfully as you can, and these days, that may just mean an old-fashioned balanced portfolio, which large institutional investors are fleeing in droves.

It's useful, when considering an asset class, to estimate the strength of the hands of your fellow owners. Are they gullible dentists, retired hardware store managers, and state public pension managers who have been sold the siren song of *past* high returns and low correlations? Is every other person you meet at a party chatting up their hedge funds and commodities and gold ETFs? Beware; their hands are weak, and the fingers attached to them will push the sell key when their investment does not live up to its billing. Contrariwise, are you and your fellow owners invested in an asset class that is either reviled or ignored, and have you and they tolerated a decade or two of sub-par performance? Then you are all likely to have strong hands, and so the investment in question will likely have both high returns and low correlations with the broad market.

This point cannot be made strongly enough: when a risky asset class becomes too popular, the fact that it is over-owned by "weak hands" means that it will simultaneously have both low expected returns and high correlations; in other words, low expected returns and high correlations go together, a fact demonstrated by most alternative asset classes over the past decade. Contrariwise, when an asset class is new and undiscovered, or has fallen from favor, it will tend to have high expected returns, and its correlation with other risky assets may well be low, because it is owned by "stronger hands." As supposedly said by J.P. Morgan, "In bear markets, stocks return to their rightful owners."

Over the past few decades, a predictable cycle of asset class behavior has arisen: Early adopters reap the initial high returns and low correlations of a novel asset class; then one or more multiple academic and trade journal articles will describe those benefits, always accompanied by plump, curvaceous two-dimensional mean-variance plots. Last come the Readers Digest versions in the mass media. (As I'm writing this, an academic piece on the salutary portfolio effects of inflation-protected emerging markets debt sits on my desk.)[14]

These mass-market articles usually sound the death knell for the asset class in question, and when their correlations rise and returns fall, as they inevitably must, the cycle begins anew. Rekenthaler's Rule, again: If the bozos know about it, it doesn't work any more.[15] (The one exception to Rekenthaler's Rule may be the value premium. By all rights, it should long since have disappeared, but shows no sign yet of doing so. Whether this is because it has deep behavioral and risk-related roots, or is in fact just starting to die, is an important question faced by all participants. In this regard, the recent spate of tech IPO catastrophes, which suggest that investors will still happily overpay for growth, is somewhat reassuring.)

One final note on the modern ease of portfolio assembly. While these days it's simple to build and rebalance a globally diversified portfolio, this facility applies only in normal times; it's rather harder during extraordinary times, both on the upside and downside. Your long term results are less the result of how well you pick assets than how well you stay the course during the bad periods, particularly if they occurred late in your investing career.

Building a widely diversified portfolio is surprisingly simple. Alas, maintaining it properly involves an appreciation of both the valuations of its individual asset class components and the character and discipline of its owners, something that the nation's largest institutional investors and their clients may not be doing particularly well.

NOTES

1   Rick Ferri, "The Curse of the Yale Model," Forbes online, 4.16/12. http://www. forbes.com/sites/rickferri/2012/04/16/the-curse-of-the-yale-model/

2   For a sampling of the early, enthusiastic treatments of the place of commodities futures in diversified portfolios, see Roger C. Gibson, Asset Allocation (Homewood, IL: Business One Irwin, 1990), 155–183, and Ernest M. Ankrim and Chris R. Hensel, "Commodities in Asset Allocation: A Real-Asset Alternative to Real Estate?" Financial Analysts Journal 49:3 (May-June, 1993): 20–29.

3   David Swensen, *Pioneering Portfolio Management* (New York: The Free Press, 2000), 114, 205–216.

4   Ibid., 256–257.

5   David Swensen, *Pioneering Portfolio Management* (New York: The Free Press, 2009).

6   Swensen (2002), 122. See also Paul M. Firstenberg, "Real Estate: The Whole Story," *Journal of Portfolio Management* 24:3 (Spring, 1988): 22–34.

7   John Y. Campbell et al., "Have Individual Stocks Become More Volatile? An Empirical Exploration of Idiosyncratic Risk," *The Journal of Finance* 56:1 (February, 2001): 1–43.

8   Martin Adeny, "Sir John Templeton," The Guardian (July 9, 2008), http://www. guardian.co.uk/business/2008/jul/10/usa accessed 9/30/12.

9   Madelon DeVoe Talley, *The Passionate Investors* (New York: Crown Publishing Inc., 1987), 66–69.

10 Adeny, ibid.

11 Charles P. Kindleberger, *Manias, Crashes, and Panics 4th Ed.* (New York: John Wiley & Sons, 2000). The table summarizing these 46 events is found in Appendix B.

12 Clifford S. Asness et al., "International Diversification Works (Eventually)," *Financial Analysts Journal* 67:3 (May-June 2011), 24–38 (quote 34).

13 The full quote comes from a slightly different context: "Saving too much money leads to a sense of nostalgic regret from a rocking chair in front of a crackling fire with a dog at your feet and a snifter of brandy at your side. Not saving enough money leads to pushing a shopping cart holding all your possessions down a wintry street and sleeping in doorways." Ben Stein and Phil DeMuth, *The Little Book of Bulletproof Investing* (Hoboken NJ: John Wiley & Sons, 2010), 138.

14 Lauren Swinkels, "Emerging Markets Inflation-Linked Bonds," *Financial Analysts Journal* 68:5 (September–October, 2012), 38–56.

15 John Rekenthaler, personal communication.

Made in the USA
San Bernardino, CA
04 December 2013